THE JUVENILE JUSTICE SYSTEM

BY DUCHESS HARRIS, JD, PHD

WITH CARLA MOONEY

Essential Library

An Imprint of Abdo Publishing | abdobooks.com

ABDOBOOKS.COM

Published by Abdo Publishing, a division of ABDO, PO Box 398166, Minneapolis, Minnesota 55439. Copyright © 2020 by Abdo Consulting Group, Inc. International copyrights reserved in all countries. No part of this book may be reproduced in any form without written permission from the publisher. Essential Library™ is a trademark and logo of Abdo Publishing.

Printed in the United States of America, North Mankato, Minnesota.
042019
092019

Interior Photos: David Goldman/AP Images, 4–5; Kayasit Sonsupap/Shutterstock Images, 8; iStockphoto, 11, 75; Denver Post/Getty Images, 15; Bettmann/ Getty Images, 16; Mile High Photo Co./Library of Congress, 18; Greg Lynch/The Journal-News/AP Images, 21, 80; Antonio Perez/Chicago Tribune/MCT/Tribune News Service/Getty Images, 26, 39, 88; Charles Rex Arbogast/AP Images, 29; Mrs. Ben B. Lindsey Collection/Library of Congress, 32; Dave Buresh/The Denver Post/ Getty Images, 34; Carlos Chavez/Los Angeles Times/Getty Images, 36; Jack Dagley Photography/Shutterstock Images, 43, 48; Brett Coomer/Houston Chronicle/AP Images, 44; Jewel Samad/AFP/Getty Images, 53; Patrick Raycraft/Hartford Courant/ AP Images, 56; Rich Legg/iStockphoto, 58; Jessica Reilly/Telegraph Herald/AP Images, 63; Paul Bilodeau/The Eagle-Tribune/AP Images, 66; Wave Break Media/ Shutterstock Images, 68; John Bazemore/AP Images, 71; Michigan Department Of Corrections/AP Images, 76; Katarzyna Bialasiewicz/iStockphoto, 87; Tony Dejak/AP Images, 91; Jessica Hill/AP Images, 94; Shutterstock Images, 98

Editor: Charly Haley
Series Designer: Dan Peluso

LIBRARY OF CONGRESS CONTROL NUMBER: 2018966013

PUBLISHER'S CATALOGING-IN-PUBLICATION DATA

Names: Harris, Duchess, author | Mooney, Carla, author.
Title: The juvenile justice system / by Duchess Harris and Carla Mooney
Description: Minneapolis, Minnesota: Abdo Publishing, 2020 | Series: History of
    crime and punishment | Includes online resources and index.
Identifiers: ISBN 9781532119217 (lib. bdg.) | ISBN 9781532173394 (ebook)
Subjects: LCSH: Juvenile justice, Administration of--United States--Juvenile
    literature. | Juvenile detention homes--United States--Juvenile
    literature. | Youth detention--Juvenile literature. | Juvenile delinquency--
    Juvenile literature.
Classification: DDC 364.360973--dc23

CONTENTS

CHAPTER ONE

WHEN CHILDREN COMMIT CRIMES

An incarcerated juvenile sits in a classroom at Metro Regional
Youth Detention Center in Georgia.

On October 11, 2014, Martha Virbitsky brought her ten-year-old son, Tristin Kurilla, to the Pennsylvania State Police barracks in Honesdale, about 140 miles (225 km) north of Philadelphia. "I killed that lady," the fifth grader confessed.[1]

A 90-year-old woman had been found dead in the boy's grandfather's home earlier that day. The grandfather, Anthony Virbitsky, shared a home with the woman and was her caretaker. Police went to the home to investigate. A few hours later, Tristin and his mother arrived at the police station. Martha Virbitsky told investigators that she believed her son had killed the elderly woman. According to a police report, Tristin's mother also said that she "has had a lot of trouble with Tristin and that he has some mental difficulties." She also indicated that he had been violent in the past.[2]

In his confession to police, Tristin admitted that he had become angry with the victim, Helen Novak, after she had yelled at him when he entered her room to ask a question. He grabbed a wooden cane and held it against her throat for several seconds and punched her in her throat and stomach. Novak died shortly after the assault. An autopsy showed Novak had suffered from blunt force trauma to her neck and concluded her death was a homicide. When asked by police whether he had wanted to kill Novak, Tristin said he had only been trying to hurt her.

CHARGED AS AN ADULT

Police charged Tristin as an adult with criminal homicide and aggravated assault, making him one of the youngest Americans to face a homicide charge. He was sent to the Wayne County Correctional Facility. At the adult prison, the ten-year-old was separated from adult offenders and supervised at all times. According to Wayne County district attorney Janine Edwards, who was responsible for filing criminal charges in the county, Pennsylvania law requires that anyone charged with criminal homicide be first charged as an adult, regardless of age, although these cases can later be moved to juvenile court. "It is not a choice I made," Edwards said, referring to the requirement to first charge Tristin as an adult. "It's not a choice the [prison] warden made. It's not a choice Pennsylvania State Police

MANDATORY TRANSFER STATUTES

Some states have mandatory transfer statutes for juvenile offenders. These are laws that require the automatic transfer of juveniles to adult criminal court for certain serious crimes, such as homicide. Mandatory transfer statutes vary by state and can be limited by crime and age. Some states require juvenile court judges to transfer children to adult court after finding probable cause. Other states require juveniles charged with certain crimes to automatically be tried in adult court. Many mandatory transfer statutes were passed during the 1990s.

made."[3] She acknowledged, however, that Tristin's young age was unusual.

Many people protested treating Tristin as an adult offender. "Social science has taught us that kids who are this young are not criminals in the same way that adults are. He has to be held accountable, yes, but in a developmentally appropriate way," says Robert Schwartz, cofounder and executive director of the Juvenile Law Center (JLC) in Philadelphia.[4] While several states require all homicide cases to begin in adult court, most include age thresholds on criminal prosecution, often between the ages of 13 and 15. However, several states, including Pennsylvania, Tennessee, and South Carolina, have no minimum age for the prosecution of a child as an adult. If tried as an adult, Tristin

Regardless of how prosecutors may feel about juvenile offenders' young age, in some states they are required by law to first charge juveniles as adults for certain crimes.

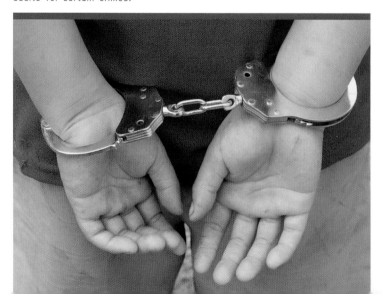

faced a minimum sentence of 25 years in prison. In addition,

a judge could increase the sentence to life.

Tristin spent several months in the adult jail awaiting trial.

During that time, he was given books, movies, and a tutor to

help him with schoolwork. At first his family was only allowed

to visit with him through a glass partition,

but eventually they were allowed physical contact so the

ten-year-old's mom could hug him. Still, the boy was scared.

"He's a ten-year-old kid away

from his family. This is not an easy

thing," said one of his lawyers,

Scott Bennett.[5]

SEPARATING JUVENILES FOR JUSTICE

The Tristin Kurilla case brought

the question of how to treat

juvenile offenders into the

national spotlight. When children

commit crimes, especially violent

offenses, how should they be

treated by the justice system?

Should they face the same

STATUS OFFENSES

Juvenile status offenses are actions that are considered crimes only because of a youth's age. If the offender were an adult, the actions would not be a crime. According to legal advice website Nolo, approximately 20 percent of all juvenile arrests are related to status offenses.[6] While status offenses vary by state, common examples include truancy (skipping school), violating curfew, underage drinking of alcohol, underage use of tobacco, and running away. Penalties for status offenses vary by state and offense. Common penalties include suspension of driver's licenses, fines, orders to attend counseling or educational programs, or being removed from the family home and placed with another relative, a foster home, or a group home.

penalties as adults? Or should children be treated differently because of their age?

Many experts argue that a separate justice system for juveniles is essential because youth offenders are much different—developmentally, emotionally, and intellectually—from adult offenders. Because of their young age, they have a much better chance to successfully rehabilitate and become contributing members of society. Judge Thomas Edwards, who served as judge of the Juvenile Court of Santa Clara County in California, says:

> *A 14-year-old is still growing, may not appreciate the consequences of that type of behavior, and is susceptible to change, at least to a higher degree than a 24-year-old is. . . . I think we have a real shot at trying to straighten out the 14-year-old, and even the people who are a little bit hard-nosed in the system, such as your average prosecutor, will sometimes grudgingly admit that, with a 14-year-old, given the proper level of accountability and the proper types of programs to change their behavior, we have a chance at salvaging these kids.*[7]

Legal experts agree that a separate juvenile justice system is important because many juveniles are not capable of making well-informed decisions about their own legal cases. Research sponsored by the MacArthur Foundation in

2003 found that more than one-third of juvenile

offenders between ages 11 and 13 have poor reasoning

about trial-related matters. In addition, it found that

children younger than 14 are less likely to understand the

long-term consequences of their decisions. "Deficiencies in

risk perception and future orientation, as well as immature

attitudes toward authority figures, may undermine

competent decision-making in ways that standard

assessments of competence to stand trial do not capture,"

the study's authors concluded.[8]

Like adults, all juveniles have a right to an attorney when facing
criminal charges.

CONFIDENTIALITY OF JUVENILE RECORDS

Once Tristin Kurilla's case was transferred to the juvenile justice system, it became confidential. Unlike adult criminal cases, juvenile court proceedings are often closed to the public, and the court records are kept confidential under state laws. This is done to limit the stigma of juvenile offenses from following youth once they become adults and try to get jobs or enroll in the military or college. In some cases, there are exceptions to juvenile court confidentiality. Some people and entities may receive access to juvenile criminal records, including parents/legal guardians, attorneys, school officials, law enforcement agencies, research organizations, and child protective agencies. Some states require a court order to inspect, receive, or copy juvenile records. In some states, law enforcement agencies are allowed to release identifying information about juvenile offenders in certain circumstances. For example, in California, law enforcement is permitted to release the names of juveniles accused of serious or violent crimes.

In addition, a juvenile suspect often relies on a parent or other family member who is not qualified to give legal advice. "Parents throw away their kids' rights too easily, not realizing that kids will often not tell the truth when adults are questioning," Schwartz says.[9] In Tristin's case, his mother brought him to the police and basically confessed for him. She waived his right to an attorney and allowed police to question him alone. During that questioning, the boy confessed. Later during an interview with the boy and his mother, police noted that the boy appeared to have trouble answering questions. The public defender assigned to Tristin's case, Bernard Brown, said that the way the boy was questioned by police was concerning.

MOVED TO JUVENILE COURT

In January 2015, a judge granted a petition filed by Tristin's attorney to move the boy's case to juvenile court. Tristin's attorney told the court that the boy has been honest and remorseful since the crime. In the juvenile justice system, Tristin will no longer be in an adult prison. Instead, he will be under supervision, potentially in a juvenile detention facility. His court-ordered supervision or detention could last for several years, up to age 21. "Tristin's very happy that the judge has given him the opportunity for treatment in the juvenile system," Bennett said. "His family is on board. I think everybody is going to be putting together a good, solid team effort for Tristin's benefit."[10] With the move to juvenile court, the rest of Tristin's case became confidential under state law.

DISCUSSION STARTERS

- How do you think children should be treated by the criminal justice system?
- Should children face the same penalties as adults for the same crimes?
- Do you think juvenile court records should be kept confidential?

CHAPTER TWO

HISTORY OF THE JUVENILE JUSTICE SYSTEM

A boy reads in his cell at Denver Juvenile Hall in Colorado in 1967.

U ntil the 1800s, children as young as seven who committed crimes in the United States could be tried in adult criminal court. If convicted, the children could be sentenced to life in prison or even sentenced to death. When deciding whether a child could be tried in adult court, the justice system considered whether the child was capable of understanding his or her actions. Children younger than seven were considered incapable of understanding their actions. This meant they could not be found guilty of a felony, which is a serious crime such as robbery, kidnapping, or murder that can be punished by jail time. Societally, children older than 14 were determined to be able to understand the difference between right and wrong. This meant they were treated as adults in the justice system.

Police arrest a boy in the late 1800s as the boy's mother asks the officers to stop.

For children between the ages of seven and 14, it wasn't always clear. Children in this age range were presumed to not be able to understand their actions, but they were assessed by the court on a case-by-case basis. If the court determined that the child could understand the difference between right and wrong, the child could be tried and convicted as an adult.

ESTABLISHING A JUVENILE COURT

During the 1800s, the treatment of children in the United States began to change. New reforms established child labor laws, mandatory education requirements, school lunches, and more. Reformers also called for the creation of special facilities for troubled youth. Reformers believed these facilities were needed to protect child offenders from adult criminals. In New York City, the New York House of Refuge opened in 1825 for juvenile delinquents. In Chicago, Illinois, the Chicago Reform School opened its doors in 1855. These facilities worked to rehabilitate child offenders to prevent them from becoming adult criminals.

In 1899, the first juvenile court in the United States was established in Cook County, Illinois. The court was founded on two main principles. First was the idea that juveniles were

Three boys meet with a juvenile court judge in Denver, Colorado, in the early 1910s.

not mature enough to take responsibility for their actions. The second principle was that because juveniles were still developing intellectually and emotionally, they could be more successfully rehabilitated than adult criminals. Today, these principles remain central to the juvenile justice system. Under the Illinois Juvenile Court Act of 1899, the court had jurisdiction over neglected, dependent, and delinquent children younger than 16. The court required youth offenders to be separated from adults in prison and banned children younger than 12 from being detained in prisons. Court records for juvenile proceedings were confidential to minimize the stigma children experienced from being in the justice system.

The idea of a separate court for juveniles quickly spread across the country. Within 25 years, most states had their own juvenile courts. Like the reform schools of the 1800s, these juvenile courts focused on rehabilitation rather than punishment. The courts tried to determine children's best interests and followed an informal approach to cases. As such, juvenile courts were required to follow few procedural rules compared with adult courts. Most cases were dealt with as noncriminal actions, called civil cases. In each case, the ultimate goal of the court was to help a juvenile offender become a responsible, lawful adult. As part of the juvenile's rehabilitation program, juvenile courts could order children to be removed from their homes and placed in juvenile reform facilities.

FORMALIZING JUVENILE JUSTICE PROCESSES

In the original, informal juvenile court process, it was common for judges to simply have conversations with accused children. No attorneys were present to represent the children in court. Proceedings often occurred behind closed doors, and the public had little knowledge about how juvenile courts operated or what happened to the young offenders. Instead of confining children in prisons with adults, the early juvenile courts often used probation, rehabilitation programs, and treatment centers to give juvenile offenders supervision and education. However, critics noted that the lack of a formal process in the juvenile justice system resulted in violations of children's rights. Unlike adults, juveniles could be detained and held in jail without a trial, a lawyer, or even being told of the charges against them.

Beginning in the 1960s, several landmark US Supreme Court cases formalized the juvenile justice system. In 1963, the Supreme Court ruled in *Gideon v. Wainwright* that every citizen, including juveniles, had the right to an attorney in a criminal proceeding. This ruling led to public defenders, who are attorneys paid by the government to represent people who can't afford to hire their own attorneys. The public defenders assigned to juvenile cases could answer any questions their young clients might have and represent them in court.

In 1966, the Supreme Court heard *Kent v. United States.* At age 14, Morris Kent first entered the juvenile justice system after an attempted purse robbery and several home break-ins. At age 16, Kent's fingerprints were discovered in the apartment of a woman who had been robbed and raped. The police detained Kent and questioned him until he admitted to the crimes. Kent's lawyer arranged for a psychiatric examination of the boy. The psychiatrist concluded that Kent suffered from severe mental illness and recommended that the boy be sent to a psychiatric hospital where he could be observed. Kent's lawyer filed motions with the court asking for the case to remain in juvenile court. The lawyer argued that Kent could be rehabilitated with proper hospital treatment. The juvenile court, however, sent the case to adult criminal court without a hearing to consider the lawyer's motions. The case ended up being appealed to the Supreme Court. In its ruling, the Supreme Court said that Kent was denied due process when he was transferred to adult criminal court without a hearing and without his attorney having access to the information the juvenile court judge used to make his decision.

In 1967, the Supreme Court established juvenile trial rights in a decision called *In re Gault*. Gerald Gault was a

A juvenile's right to an attorney is intended to ensure he has someone to help navigate the complicated criminal justice system.

15-year-old boy in Arizona who was accused of making indecent phone calls to a neighbor. He was also on probation for stealing a wallet with another boy. When the neighbor called police, officers took Gault into custody and held him in jail overnight without notifying his parents. Before his court hearing the next day, Gault and his parents were not notified of the specific charges against him. He was not advised of his rights to remain silent or to have an attorney present. No sworn witnesses were called, and there was no written record of the proceedings. Even the neighbor who had complained about the phone call was not present. At the end of the hearings, the juvenile court judge sent Gault to Arizona State Industrial School until age 21, a period of six years. Had Gault been an adult convicted of the same crime, he would have faced only a maximum fine of $50 and up to two months in jail. Gault's parents argued for their son's release, saying he had been denied due process of law and his constitutional right to a fair trial had been violated. Ultimately, the Supreme Court heard the case. In its decision, the court sided with the Gaults and ruled that the boy's rights had been violated. This decision paved the way for children charged in juvenile court to have many of the same due process rights as adults, including the right to an attorney, the right to question witnesses, and the right against self-incrimination.

After *Gault*, the Supreme Court recognized additional constitutional rights for children in the juvenile justice system, including the right to have charges proven beyond a reasonable doubt and the right against double jeopardy, which refers to prosecuting a person twice for the same offense. In 1971, the court ruled that juvenile court cases were not guaranteed to have jury trials. However, several states have their own laws to provide juvenile defendants with the right to a jury trial.

JUVENILE JUSTICE AND DELINQUENCY PREVENTION ACT

In 1974, the US Congress passed the Juvenile Justice and Delinquency Prevention Act (JJDPA). The law coordinates federal efforts to improve state juvenile justice systems and focus on education and rehabilitation. The act provides for a nationwide juvenile justice planning and advisory system, as well as federal funding for improvements in state and local juvenile justice programs. It also established a federal agency, the Office of Juvenile Justice and Delinquency Prevention, which supports state and local systems.

TOUGH-ON-CRIME POLICIES

In the late 1980s and early 1990s, an increase in juvenile crime rates led many state legislators to pass what were known as tough-on-crime policies. Legislators believed that harsher punishments would deter juvenile crime. States passed laws that allowed prosecutors to more easily transfer youth from the juvenile justice system to adult criminal court. In some cases, this led to juveniles being sentenced to life in prison without the possibility of parole or even sentenced to death. Tough-on-crime state laws placed juvenile offenders in prisons with adult criminals and exposed them to increased danger and abuses, similar to those they had faced nearly a century earlier before the juvenile courts were created.

Since the 1990s, juvenile crime rates have decreased. According to a Pew Charitable Trusts research report, juvenile violent crime arrests, including arrests for murder, manslaughter, aggravated assault, and robbery, fell 49 percent from 2006 to 2015.[1] Even so, harsh penalties for juvenile offenders still remain in many states. Because of this, some experts believe that the primary goal of the juvenile

DIFFERENCES IN JUVENILE AND ADULT JUSTICE

The US criminal justice system treats juveniles and adults differently in many ways, such as:

- When arrested by law enforcement, adults can post bond, which means paying a set amount of money to get out of jail while waiting for their cases to be heard in court. Juveniles detained by police don't have the right to post bond.
- Adults have the right to a jury trial. In most cases, juveniles don't have this right. Instead, a judge will hear the evidence in a hearing and will make a ruling as to whether the juvenile committed a delinquent act.
- The main purpose of the adult criminal justice system is punishment. The courts attempt to impose a punishment that will make it less likely for the offender to commit the same crime in the future. In contrast, the juvenile justice system's primary goal is rehabilitation. The court often uses parole and probation to direct juvenile offenders on a new path and keep them out of trouble in the future.

justice system—to rehabilitate young offenders so they can become productive, law-abiding adults—has been lost to the punishment approach of the adult criminal justice system.

THE MODERN JUVENILE JUSTICE SYSTEM

Today, people younger than 18 accused of a delinquent or criminal act are generally processed by the juvenile justice system. While similar to the adult criminal justice system in many ways, the juvenile justice system is based on the belief that youth are significantly different from adults, both in their level of responsibility and their ability to be rehabilitated. Therefore, the primary goal of the juvenile justice system is to balance the rehabilitation and treatment of young offenders with maintaining public safety. Keeping the goal of rehabilitation in mind, reform efforts are underway in many jurisdictions that still have harsh penalties for juvenile offenders.

When children enter the juvenile justice system, they are typically taken into custody and held at a detention facility. The system is supposed to move cases along quickly, so court hearings are generally scheduled as soon as possible. In juvenile court, defendants are represented by an attorney. Often their cases will be heard and decided by a judge. This is called a bench trial, as opposed to a jury trial, in which the case is decided by a jury. If a juvenile is found guilty, the court determines the best way to rehabilitate the juvenile.

Juvenile courts have several legal options that focus on treatment and rehabilitation of the child while still considering public safety. In some cases, this involves removing juvenile offenders from their homes and placing them in institutions for rehabilitation. This may include short-term detention, time in a residential treatment facility, or long-term incarceration in a secure juvenile facility.

Juvenile courts may also order youth to participate in community-based alternatives, which allow the juveniles to remain at home with their families, continue attending school, and participate in a wider variety of rehabilitative programs. One community-based alternative is probation.

An Illinois Department of Juvenile Justice Center staff member escorts a group of incarcerated juveniles to their classroom at the center. Education is part of the juvenile justice system's rehabilitative approach.

While on probation, a juvenile is supervised by an officer of the court and must follow strict rules. These rules may include requirements to take drug tests, go to school, and attend treatments such as counseling. Courts may order juveniles to perform community service, such as picking up trash or serving at a soup kitchen. The court may also order juveniles to participate in therapy if the judge believes it will help them avoid delinquency in the future.

Unlike adult criminal proceedings, juvenile court hearings are often closed to the public, and juvenile records remain confidential. These measures protect children in the juvenile justice system from the stigma of being labeled juvenile offenders long after their cases are closed. However, in recent years, juvenile justice records have become more accessible and, in many states, are not automatically sealed when the youth becomes an adult.

DISCUSSION STARTERS

- Do you think juveniles should have the right to a jury trial? Why or why not?
- Do you think harsher punishments deter juvenile crime?
- Is there still a stigma attached to youth who are involved in the juvenile justice system? How can this affect them in the future?

CHAPTER THREE

JUVENILE
INCARCERATION

Tone Knight sits in his cell at the Juvenile Medium Security Facility in New Jersey in 1999. He told a news reporter that his fellow inmates were misunderstood.

According to the Prison Policy Initiative, nearly 53,000 youth in the United States are held on any given day in facilities away from their homes. Nearly 10 percent are held in adult jails or prisons.[1] These youth are incarcerated as a result of their involvement in the juvenile or criminal justice systems.

HISTORY OF JUVENILE INCARCERATION

Juvenile incarceration has a long history in the United States. In the 1700s and 1800s, courts punished juvenile offenders by confining them in jails and prisons. There were few juvenile facilities, so youth were often locked up with adult criminals and people with mental illnesses in large, overcrowded jails and prisons. Many of these juveniles were imprisoned for noncriminal behavior, such as being considered rowdy or out of control, because cities had no other places to send them.

In 1817, concerns about placing delinquent and abandoned children in adult prisons led to the formation of

RACE MATTERS

Black, Hispanic, and Native American juveniles are disproportionately incarcerated. The difference is particularly noticeable for black males and Native American females. While less than 14 percent of Americans younger than 18 are black, they represent 43 percent of boys and 34 percent of girls in juvenile facilities. Native Americans are only 1 percent of US juveniles, but they make up 3 percent of girls and 1.5 percent of boys in juvenile facilities.[2]

the Society for the Prevention of Pauperism in New York City. The society's members argued that cities needed separate youth facilities. In 1825, the New York House of Refuge was established. It was the first facility designed to house impoverished and delinquent youth. Similar facilities opened in cities across the country over the next two decades. These first houses of refuge were large, multistory institutions located in urban areas.

In the early 1800s, houses of refuge held increasing numbers of children. They quickly faced the same issues as adult prisons—overcrowding, poor living conditions, and abuse by staff. In addition, social reformers in the United States argued for a greater government role in the education of all children. This movement led to a new type of institution, the reform school, which focused more on education and rehabilitation for delinquent children. One of the country's first reform schools, the Lyman Reform School for Boys, opened in 1846 in Westborough, Massachusetts. At the Lyman School, juveniles raised livestock, grew vegetables, sewed clothes, and built many of the structures on the school property. The school, like many reform schools, recognized that youth had a better chance of being rehabilitated than adult offenders and therefore should be treated differently than adults. Reform schools, also called training and industrial schools, became an integral part of America's juvenile justice system. Today, reform schools are still part of the juvenile justice system. Often called youth correctional institutions, modern reform schools typically hold a large number of youth in a regimented, prisonlike facility.

COTTAGE INSTITUTIONS

While reform schools were an improvement over sending juveniles to adult prisons, conditions in these facilities were often less than ideal. Many schools faced problems of overcrowding and disease. In some areas, the prisonlike barracks of reform schools and houses of refuge

A classroom at a boys' reform school in the early 1900s

were gradually replaced by smaller cottage institutions in the mid-1800s. In cottage institutions, married supervisors called house parents lived with about 20 to 30 children.[3] Cottage house parents provided parental supervision and counsel to the young residents. Some cottages were built on large rural campuses. Others were located at older correctional facilities or state hospital sites such as the Minnesota Home School in Sauk Centre, Minnesota, and the Mount View School in Golden, Colorado. Early cottage programs were positive. For many youth, the surrogate family formed by the cottage institution was an improvement over having no family at all. The cottage system is still used by some private juvenile facilities, such as Girls and Boys Town in Nebraska and the Le Roy Boys Home in California. Modern labor laws limit the working hours of house parents to 40 to 48 hours per week. Therefore, cottage institutions are also staffed by day counselors and other support staff.

MODERN JUVENILE FACILITIES

Today, tens of thousands of juveniles are incarcerated in the United States on any given day. According to the Prison Policy Initiative, nearly two out of every three confined juveniles are held in the most restrictive, correctional-style

A classroom at a juvenile court facility in Denver, Colorado, in 1967

facilities. Some are housed in adult jails and prisons. Others are in juvenile correctional facilities such as detention centers, long-term secure facilities, and temporary facilities called reception and diagnostic centers. In these correctional facilities, 99.7 percent of youth are restricted by locked doors, gates, or fences. Sixty percent are in large facilities built to hold more than 50 people.[4]

The largest number of incarcerated youth are in detention centers, which are similar to jails in the adult criminal justice system. Operated by local authorities, detention centers temporarily hold juvenile defendants while they wait for court hearings or sentencing.[5]

Once they are sentenced, many juvenile offenders are confined in long-term secure facilities. These facilities, often called training schools, are comparable to adult prisons.

At long-term secure facilities, hundreds of youth are confined behind razor wire fences. Inside, some juveniles are put in solitary confinement or restrained with mechanical restraints.

Reception and diagnostic centers are often located near long-term secure facilities. These centers evaluate youth sentenced by the juvenile courts and assign them to long-term secure correctional facilities. Like detention centers, reception and diagnostic centers are meant to be temporary. Still, more than half of the juveniles in these facilities stay for more than 90 days. One in eight youth in these centers stays for more than a year.[6]

In addition to correctional-style or prisonlike facilities, some youth are confined in residential-style facilities, which are generally less restrictive than correctional facilities. They vary significantly and include military-style boot camps, wilderness or ranch camps, shelters, or group homes where residents can go to school

COST OF INCARCERATION

Incarcerating juveniles is expensive. According to a 2015 report by the Justice Policy Institute, the cost of incarceration for a single inmate averages $401 per day and $146,302 per year in a state's high-cost juvenile facilities.[7] In addition, the financial costs of incarceration continue to increase after a juvenile is released. When these juveniles lose out on earnings as a result of struggling to hold jobs, communities lose out on tax revenue. Incarcerated youth dealing with long-term mental and physical effects from incarceration incur more expenses in the health care, Medicaid, and Medicare systems.

Incarcerated youth at the Juvenile Justice Center in Ventura, California, participate in programs to learn labor skills as part of their rehabilitation.

or work. Although they are considered residential, 70 percent of these facilities still lock residents in their sleeping rooms and have a variety of locked doors and gates intended to confine the residents.[8]

LOCKED UP FOR MINOR CRIMES

Many youth are incarcerated because they committed serious offenses and the courts determined that they are a danger to the community. However, many others are locked up in juvenile facilities for minor offenses. According to the Prison Policy Initiative, almost one-quarter of all youth in juvenile facilities are incarcerated because of technical violations (18 percent) or status offenses (5 percent). Technical violations include not reporting to a probation officer, failing to finish community service, or not following through with court-ordered referrals. Even though these offenses are minor, they can result in a long confinement in a very restrictive juvenile facility. Nearly 50 percent of youth held for status offenses are incarcerated for more than 90 days, while almost 25 percent are held in the most restrictive, correctional-style juvenile facilities.[9]

Some youth who have committed minor crimes or status offenses are even held in juvenile facilities before they are sentenced. According to a 2018 report by the Prison Policy Initiative, more than 9,000 youth—approximately one in five juvenile offenders—are locked up in detention centers waiting for a court hearing. Detention centers are meant to be temporary places to hold youth who are at a high risk of reoffending. However, many juveniles are detained simply for technical violations of probation or status offenses. An additional 6,500 youth are being held awaiting sentencing or placement.[10]

CALL FOR TOUGHER PUNISHMENTS

While many people support reducing the number of juveniles incarcerated, others believe that offenders should be punished more severely. William Otis, a law professor at Georgetown University and former federal prosecutor, argues that harsher punishments for both juveniles and adults are the best ways to reduce crime. To illustrate his point, Otis refers to the case of Wendell Callahan. After being arrested at age 17, Callahan was sentenced to a long prison term for drug crimes. After ten years in prison, Callahan earned an early release. Only two years later, he murdered his ex-girlfriend and her two children. According to Otis, the case highlights why tougher punishments are necessary. Former US attorney general Jeff Sessions also advocated for harsher punishments in 2017. He instructed federal prosecutors to seek harsher criminal sentencing, especially in cases involving drugs and violence.

HARMFUL EFFECTS OF INCARCERATION

Incarceration can have serious, harmful effects on a person of any age. But for juveniles who are still developing mentally and physically, the damage can be greater. When youth are removed from their homes, schools, and communities, they lose sources of social and emotional support. Without these support systems, they develop higher rates of depression, anxiety, and other mental health conditions, according to the National Juvenile Defender Center. Incarcerated youth also have fewer educational opportunities. This problem continues after their release. Children who have been incarcerated often have trouble keeping up once they return to school. Sixty percent choose not to return at all or drop out within five months.[11] The combination of increased mental health problems and lack of education can make it difficult to maintain a job. As a result, these youth make less money and may end up living in poverty.

According to a study published in the journal *Pediatrics* in 2017, people incarcerated as juveniles may have worse physical and mental health as adults compared to those who were not incarcerated. In addition, the harmful effect on health increases with the amount of time a person is

Some researchers and advocates say that juvenile incarceration, even with the goal of rehabilitation, is still more harmful than helpful to youth.

incarcerated. The study found that participants who were in the juvenile justice system for less than a month were 41 percent more likely to have depression symptoms as adults compared to those who were never incarcerated. Juveniles who were incarcerated between one to 12 months experienced a 48 percent increased risk of general health problems as adults. And study participants who were incarcerated as juveniles for more than a year were nearly three times more likely to have functional limitations such as difficulty climbing stairs and four times more likely to have depression symptoms. "Like most things in life, the experiences they have as a young person seem to carry over into their adult years," says public health expert Ralph DiClemente.[12]

EFFORTS TO REDUCE JUVENILE INCARCERATION

According to data from the federal Office of Juvenile Justice and Delinquency Prevention, the juvenile commitment rate, which is the share of youth in the juvenile justice system who are in residential facilities, dropped by 50 percent between 2006 and 2015.[14] This decline in juvenile incarceration comes at the same time as a drop in violent crime committed by juveniles over the same period.

Many states have decreased the number of juveniles incarcerated by placing only the most serious and repeating offenders into residential facilities. These reforms are based on a growing amount of research showing that placing juvenile offenders in residential facilities fails to produce better outcomes than other community-based programs.

In addition, juveniles who are incarcerated are often exposed to violence and abuse. According to a 2015 report by the Annie E. Casey Foundation, systemic maltreatment of youth has been documented in juvenile correctional facilities in 29 states, with substantial evidence of maltreatment found in three additional states.[13] Systemic maltreatment includes violence, physical or sexual abuse by staff, and the excessive use of isolation or physical restraints. For example, in Arkansas, staff at the Yell County Juvenile Detention Center were ordered in 2014 to stop restraining youth and stop making them wear a motorcycle helmet with duct tape covering the face shield that was decorated with a hand-drawn, cartoon face. These youth were forced to sit upright for hours at a time, with their legs restrained and arms handcuffed behind their backs while they sat in almost complete darkness. In addition, nearly 10 percent of confined youth report being sexually abused by staff or other youth in their facilities.[15]

GETTING INTO TROUBLE AGAIN

Incarcerating juveniles may make it more likely that they will reoffend in the future. In many areas of the country, 50 percent to 75 percent of incarcerated juveniles will reoffend within three years of being released.[16] "We have to recognize that incarceration of youth per se is toxic," says Barry Krisberg, former president of the National Council on Crime and Delinquency, "so we need to reduce incarceration of young people to the very small, dangerous few. And we've got to recognize that if we lock up a lot of kids, it's going to increase crime."[17]

DISCUSSION STARTERS

- In what circumstances do you believe juvenile offenders should be committed to secure facilities?
- What do you think would be an effective alternative to juvenile incarceration?
- Do you think juveniles should be locked up for status offenses and minor crimes?

CHAPTER FOUR

GENDER DISPARITIES

A police officer arrests a juvenile girl.

C reating the juvenile justice system protected the rights of youth and focused on rehabilitation to help them become law-abiding, productive adults. However, many of the juvenile justice system's policies and programs were developed for boys, who were once the large majority of juveniles in the system. These policies and programs often fail to meet the needs of girls, whose involvement in the system has steadily increased over the years. "While pockets of effective programming for girls have been created, the juvenile justice system as a whole has yet to develop consistent gender-specific strategies that will address the critical needs of adolescent girls," says Chandlee Johnson Kuhn, a former family court chief judge in Delaware.[1]

Research shows an increasing number of girls are entering the US juvenile justice system, which may not be prepared to meet their needs.

Judge Nikita V. Harmon
176th District Criminal Court

Advocates have called for change in the juvenile justice system to address gender differences in order to best serve all youth, regardless of gender.

DIFFERENT EXPECTATIONS AND TREATMENT

Since the earliest days of the juvenile justice system, boys and girls have been treated differently. When the first juvenile court was established in 1899, it defined *delinquent* as any person younger than 16 who had broken a city law or ordinance. The court applied an additional definition of delinquency to girls that included "incorrigibility, association with immoral persons, vagrancy, frequent attendance at pool halls or saloons, other debauched conduct, and use of profane language."[2] Boys were not held to these stricter standards. This difference was based on gender norms, or how society typically believes people of each gender should behave. "Unlike decisions around boys' delinquency, which centered on a concern for public safety, the behaviors that characterized girls' criminalization had more to do with preventing girls from being sexually promiscuous, protecting girls from victimization, and ensuring that young women and girls' behavior was socially acceptable," according to a March 2018 report from the Georgetown Juvenile Justice

GENDER AND RACE

Girls of color are impacted even more by gender differences in the juvenile justice system. Black girls are 14 percent of the general population, yet they make up 34 percent of detained and committed girls. Native American girls make up only 1 percent of the youth population, but they constitute 3 percent of girls detained and committed.[5]

Initiative and the Rights4Girls nonprofit organization.[3]

More than 100 years later, there are still differences in how boys and girls are treated by the juvenile justice system. Today numerous studies have found that girls are more likely to enter the juvenile justice system for status offenses such as truancy, running away, or incorrigibility.[4] In addition, gender norms dictate that girls should be cooperative and compliant, increasing the likelihood that those who don't behave this way will be pushed into the juvenile justice system. Once in the juvenile justice system, the specific struggles and needs of girls are more likely to be dismissed or overlooked.

Research points to several reasons why the juvenile system continues to treat girls differently than boys. First, many people in the justice system believe in the stereotype that girls need to be protected from themselves and others. Secondly, the system has developed a habit of using locked confinement to deal with girls over alternative options. "Decisions to arrest, detain, and maintain girls' involvement in the juvenile justice system can often be attributed to paternalism on the part of system players who believe that girls who engage in certain behaviors must be subjected to more control and supervision for their own protection," write researchers from the Georgetown Juvenile Justice Initiative report.[6]

INCREASING REPRESENTATION

In recent years, the number of girls entering the juvenile justice system has increased significantly. According to the 2018 Rights4Girls report, the number of girls arrested increased by 45 percent between 1992 and 2013. The proportion of court cases involving girls increased by 40 percent.[7] Similar increases have also occurred in the proportion of girls placed on probation and sent to residential facilities.

Several studies have shown that the increase in girls' involvement in the juvenile justice system isn't because their behavior has changed. There is no evidence to support the idea

SEXUAL ORIENTATION

Girls in the LGBTQ (lesbian, gay, bisexual, transgender, and queer) community are overrepresented in the juvenile justice system. Lesbian, gay, and bisexual youth are about 7 to 9 percent of the general population, but they are 20 percent of youth in juvenile justice facilities. Specifically, about 40 percent of girls in juvenile justice facilities identify as lesbian, gay, or bisexual, compared with 3.2 percent of boys in juvenile justice facilities.[8]

Research shows that girls are more likely to be arrested for minor, nonviolent offenses.

that girls are committing more crimes or becoming more violent. Instead, girls have become more likely to commit status offenses, especially running away. Researchers believe that because law enforcement is increasingly enforcing nonserious offenses, more girls are entering the system. "Because girls are more likely than boys to be arrested and detained for minor offenses, this practice has a disparate impact on girls," write researchers from the 2018 Rights4Girls report.[9]

HISTORY OF ABUSE AND TRAUMA

Girls in the juvenile justice system often have similar

backgrounds. Many have experienced poverty, an unstable

family life, and neglect. They often have experienced

sexual, physical, or emotional abuse. These experiences

can contribute to behaviors that land people in the juvenile

justice system. Girls who experience abuse may run away to

escape, while others skip school or turn to drugs and alcohol

to cope. These behaviors are some of the most common

crimes for which girls are arrested. Other times, girls get in

trouble for getting into fights, which may be a response to

abuse in the home. "If a girl has a history of violence, we

know that's a symptom of trauma," says activist Nona Jones.[10]

The US Attorney General's Task Force on Children Exposed to

TRYING TO SURVIVE

Girls who are homeless or living in poverty are more likely to be in the juvenile justice system. Seventy-eight percent of homeless youth included in a 2017 study by the Administration on Children, Youth and Families had had at least one contact with law enforcement. Nearly 44 percent had been detained in a juvenile detention center, jail, or prison.[11] Girls who don't have a stable place to live often turn to survival behaviors such as sleeping in public places, entering places without permission, or stealing to pay for food and other expenses. These behaviors can lead to arrests for loitering, trespassing, and theft. Some homeless girls have run away to escape abuse at home. In addition, girls who don't have a stable place to live are also at a higher risk of being exploited and lured into prostitution, which may lead to being arrested and becoming involved with the juvenile justice system.

Violence concluded in 2012 that childhood trauma is linked to becoming involved in the juvenile justice system.

Across the country, 73 percent of girls in the juvenile justice system have experienced physical or sexual abuse at some point in their lives. Girls are four times more likely than boys in the system to have experienced childhood sexual abuse.[12] In fact, a 2015 study found that sexual abuse is one of the main predictors of whether a girl will enter the juvenile justice system. "Our girls, and especially our girls at the margins, are suffering, and what the study shows is how violence is part of their lives and how the response is criminalization," says Malika Saada Saar, executive director of the Human Rights Project for Girls.[13]

Once in the juvenile justice system, girls can get stuck. The system falls short of identifying and treating the violence and trauma at the root of their behavior. In addition, being confined in juvenile facilities may trigger girls' trauma and expose them to additional sexual victimization at the hands of staff or other inmates. "When law enforcement views girls as perpetrators, and when their cases are not dismissed or diverted but sent deeper into the justice system, the cost is twofold: Girls' abusers are shielded from accountability, and the trauma that is the underlying cause of the behavior is not

addressed," write the 2015 study's researchers.[14]

EFFORTS FOR CHANGE

To address girls' specific needs, several states are changing

their juvenile justice practices. In Florida and Connecticut,

legislators have mandated the development of

gender-specific programs to focus on helping girls. In

Hawaii and California, the justice system created girls' courts

that coordinate with gender-specific programs for youth

offenders. These programs include family involvement,

therapy, and peer support. Illinois and Maryland have passed

laws that require schools to respond to students' disruptive

behavior by teaching social skills instead of expelling

students and calling in law enforcement to make arrests.

DISCUSSION STARTERS

- What type of gender-specific program would you create to help girls in the juvenile justice system? How would it address the needs of girls?
- How are the needs of girls different than those of boys in the juvenile justice system?
- Do you notice differences in gender norms and behavior expectations for girls and boys in your school? In your community?

CHAPTER FIVE

RACE AND JUVENILE JUSTICE

A young activist is arrested during widespread protests against police brutality in Ferguson, Missouri, in 2014.

I n recent years, a decline in juvenile crime and reforms in the juvenile justice system have led to an overall decrease in the youth incarceration rate. According to a 2016 report from the Sentencing Project, a nonprofit advocacy organization, the rate of youth committed to juvenile facilities dropped by 47 percent between 2003 and 2013.[1] Yet not all children are equally benefiting from these declines. Children of color remain far more likely to be sent to juvenile facilities than their white peers. Approximately one-third of adolescents in the United States are people of color, but two-thirds of incarcerated youth are people of color.[2] Youth of color are disproportionately represented at nearly every point in the juvenile justice system, from arrest through incarceration.

FEDERAL EFFORT TO SHRINK THE RACIAL GAP

In 1988, Congress amended the Juvenile Justice and Delinquency Prevention Act of 1974 to address the overrepresentation of youth of color in secure commitment facilities. Under the amendment, the federal Office of Juvenile Justice and Delinquency Prevention has provided grants and training to local juvenile courts and law enforcement agencies. In return, the states receiving this federal funding must gather data on racial inequality, explore the reasons why it occurs, and develop and implement solutions to reduce it.

ACROSS THE SYSTEM

The United States has the largest criminal justice system in the world. However, racial disparity exists throughout the system at all levels. According to a 2018 report by the Sentencing Project, black people are more likely to be arrested, convicted, and given long sentences than white people. This disparity exists in part because of long-standing institutional racism, which occurs when government organizations, schools, banks, courts, and other institutions treat a group of people unfavorably because of their race.

The juvenile justice system is no exception. People of color are disproportionately involved in the juvenile system from their first contacts with law enforcement. Between 2003 and 2013, overall juvenile arrest rates dropped 34 percent, according to the Sentencing Project. This decline in arrests carried across all major categories of offenses. Yet over the same period, black youth remained much more likely to be

THE SCOTTSBORO BOYS

In 1931, police arrested nine black teenage boys after a fight on a train traveling near Scottsboro, Alabama. When police questioned two white women on the train, they falsely accused the boys of rape. Police arrested the boys, and within two weeks, an all-white jury convicted them. Eight were sentenced to death, while the youngest, who was 13, was sentenced to life in prison. Activists launched a national campaign to free the boys and fight racism in the justice system. They organized speeches, parades, and demonstrations to rally the public. Eventually, one accuser admitted she had been pressured into making the false accusation.

In 1932, the US Supreme Court overturned the Scottsboro convictions, ruling the boys were denied their right to an attorney, which violated their right to due process under the Fourteenth Amendment. In 1935, the Supreme Court overturned the state's guilty verdicts again, ruling the exclusion of black people on the jury rolls denied the defendants a fair trial. The Scottsboro Boys' case had a lasting effect on the US justice system and helped fuel the civil rights movement a few decades later.

arrested. Black youth were 129 percent more likely to be arrested than white youth in 2013. This was an increase from 2003, when black youth were 85 percent more likely to be arrested than white youth.[3] Despite the difference in arrest rates, the offenses committed by youth of different races are nearly identical. Researchers have found that youth of color and white youth are approximately as likely to commit the same offenses—getting into fights, carrying weapons, stealing property, using and selling illicit drugs, and status offenses. "Those similarities are not reflected in arrest rates; black teenagers are far more likely than their white peers to be arrested across a range of offenses, a vital step toward

Black youth are generally more likely than white youth to receive harsher sentences in court because of racial disparities in the criminal justice system.

creating the difference in commitments," write the authors of a report from the Sentencing Project.[4] While some studies show that black youth are more likely than white youth to commit violent crimes, those crimes make up less than 5 percent of juvenile arrests.[5] Therefore, the violent crime rates do not explain the difference in juvenile arrests by race.

Once a youth is arrested, racial disparity continues in the juvenile justice system. After arrest, some youth are able to avoid formal processing in court by being directed into a pretrial diversion program. These programs often require youth to participate in mandatory counseling, community service, or educational programs. They may also be required to pay for any damage they caused to victims. Youth who voluntarily complete diversion program requirements can have their charges dismissed. In addition, diversion programs help rehabilitate delinquent youth by teaching responsibility and coping skills. However, white youth are more likely to be directed into pretrial diversion programs than children of color. "These diversion approaches are available in communities that have resources," says B. K. Elizabeth Kim, a social work professor at the University of Southern California.[6] This leaves a disproportionate number of youth of color to have their cases heard in court. Once in court, black youth are more likely than white youth to be found delinquent by a judge. In addition, youth of color are disproportionately sentenced to secure juvenile facilities instead of being put on probation.

At each step of the process, youth of color are more likely to be in the juvenile justice system than their white peers. "Youth of color are more likely to be arrested once they come in contact with the police than white youth, they're more likely to be charged after an arrest, they're more likely to be transferred to an adult court, they're more likely to be sentenced more harshly," Kim says. "So at every point . . . they're just more likely to be pulled into the system than having other opportunities."[7]

Black youth, especially boys, are more likely to experience discrimination from law enforcement and the criminal justice system starting at a young age.

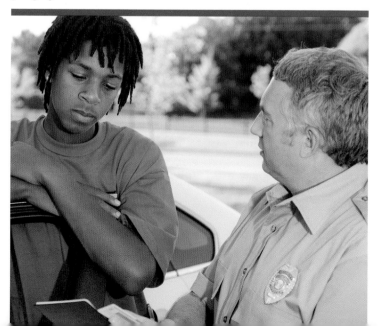

WHAT CAUSES RACIAL DISPARITY?

Many experts who have studied race and the juvenile justice system believe that there is no single reason why youth of color are more involved with the system at every point compared to their white peers. Instead, experts believe that several factors contribute to this disparity. One of the main factors is racial bias among officials in the juvenile justice system such as police officers, probation officers, and judges. Officials with this bias treat youth of color more harshly than white youth. For example, police might stop youth of color more frequently than white youth, even though they're engaging in the same behavior. This unequal treatment may be intentional or unintentional.

Location may also play a role in the juvenile justice system's racial disparity. Youth who live in racially diverse cities may be treated differently by juvenile justice officials than their peers from mostly white neighborhoods. Similarly, differences may arise in the treatment of youth from wealthy versus poor neighborhoods. In addition, racial stereotyping may be more common in certain areas. Negative stereotypes about a racial group can affect how individual children are treated by police and other juvenile justice professionals.

Youth of color may also have less access to services and programs that prevent juvenile delinquency. This may be affected by a child's surrounding community, income level, education level, and beliefs about mental health care. For example, because access to mental health care is often limited for youth of color, these children may be more at risk for engaging in delinquent behavior when they are not receiving the care they need. In comparison, white youth are more likely to have access to and to use mental health care, which can help prevent future delinquent behavior.

IMPROVING POLICE-YOUTH RELATIONSHIPS

To reduce racial disparities in arrests, many communities are conducting training programs for all law enforcement officers. These programs are designed to help police develop skills and cultural awareness that will help them have more positive interactions with all youth, especially youth of color. For example, in Pennsylvania, police receive training on adolescent development, youth culture, and how environment impacts adolescent behavior. The Pennsylvania program also brings police and youth together for annual forums to connect and discuss issues.

EFFORTS TO REDUCE RACIAL DISPARITY

To reduce racial disparities in the juvenile justice system, many states have implemented reforms to promote equal treatment for children of all races. For example, several states have passed laws that require cities to establish community-based policing or have funded programs that support it. Community-based policing uses the idea that the police and community members can work together to reduce crime and solve other safety issues. In addition, at least 30 states have passed laws that define and ban racial profiling.[8] Racial profiling occurs when law enforcement target people based on race or ethnicity, regardless of whether the targeting is intentional.

Many states have also started improving their data collection and analysis processes to help identify and eliminate inherent bias in the criminal justice system. For example, by collecting and analyzing data about the state's juvenile justice process, Connecticut identified that youth of color were being transferred to adult court at significantly higher rates. The state then implemented training for all prosecutors to help them better understand racial bias and how they could help reduce it.

DISCUSSION STARTERS

- How does racial profiling affect the racial disparity in the juvenile justice system?
- What can communities do to reduce racial disparity in the juvenile justice system?
- How can collecting data about the juvenile justice process help reduce the racial gap?

CHAPTER SIX

TRIED AS ADULTS

Juvenile offenders face more-serious punishments when they're tried as adults.

n 2007, 16-year-old Marquis McKenzie stood handcuffed before a juvenile judge in a Florida courtroom. McKenzie was accused of armed robbery, allegedly stealing a wallet and cell phone. The judge announced the charges and said he couldn't hear the teen's case in juvenile court because state law gave the prosecutor the right to direct file the case and transfer the teen to adult court without the judge's permission. "You're being direct filed," the judge told McKenzie. "You understand what I'm saying? You're being charged as an adult now."[1] A decade later, McKenzie still remembered his mother crying out from the courtroom seats and begging the judge to keep her son's case in juvenile court. "I had never been in that situation. I had gotten in trouble, but I had never gotten arrested," he said in 2017. "I just knew it was going to be a hell of a ride from there."[2] The transfer to adult court meant that McKenzie could no longer take advantage of the rehabilitative services offered by Florida's juvenile justice system. Instead, he was sentenced to ten years in the juvenile section of one of Florida's medium-security prisons.

Like McKenzie, an estimated 250,000 youth in the United States are tried, sentenced, or incarcerated as adults every year, according to the National Juvenile Justice Network.[3]

In the 1990s, the practice of charging youth as adults in criminal court increased in response to a spike in youth crime. During the 1990s, 49 states changed their laws to lower the age at which youth could be tried and sentenced as adults.[4] This increased the number of teens in adult prisons. "That was a 'get tough' era in the United States," says Florida State University criminologist Carter Hay. "That was a time when there was a lot of concern about juvenile crime. There was a lot of media attention to the idea that there were these juvenile super-predators who were just a real threat to public safety."[5] As a result, the number of youth in adult jails increased by nearly 230 percent between 1990 and 2010, according to the Sentencing Project.[6] While the number of youth confined in adult jails and prisons peaked in 1999 and has declined since then, the number of youth in adult facilities is still higher than in 1990. In 2018, about 10 percent of confined youth were in an adult prison or jail, according to the Prison Policy Initiative, an advocacy research group.[7]

WHAT IS DIRECT FILE?

Direct file occurs when a state gives prosecutors the power to file charges against a juvenile directly in adult criminal court. When prosecutors direct file a case in adult court, they override any juvenile or family court jurisdiction in a case. In states that allow direct file, prosecutors are allowed to determine where to charge a juvenile, which determines what possible sentences the juvenile may face if convicted. As of 2018, 12 states and Washington, DC, permitted direct file.[8]

A 15-year-old accused of first-degree murder is escorted into court by police. Teens charged with high-level, violent crimes may be more likely to be tried as adults.

TREATMENT DIFFERS BY STATE

The way juveniles are treated by the justice system varies by state. Every state sets a maximum age a person is considered a juvenile in court. Once people exceed the maximum age, they are considered adults in the criminal justice system. They are sent to adult criminal court, regardless of the level of criminal charges filed against them. In most states, 17 is the maximum age for a defendant's case to be heard in juvenile court. Five states—Georgia, Michigan, Missouri, Texas, and Wisconsin—set 16 as the maximum age for the juvenile justice system. For many years, New York and North Carolina had 15 as the maximum age for juvenile court. In these states, a person age 16 or 17 who was charged with any criminal offense could be tried in adult criminal court. This changed in 2017, when both New York and North Carolina passed legislation to raise the age of juvenile court jurisdiction to 17.

In addition, many states have laws that allow prosecutors to transfer a juvenile case to the adult criminal court for certain crimes. As a result, juveniles younger than the maximum age for juvenile court can be transferred and tried in adult court. Typically, a case can be transferred from juvenile court to adult court in one of three ways: judicial waiver, prosecutorial discretion laws, or statutory rule. In judicial waiver, the juvenile court judge sends the case to adult court. In doing so, the judge takes into account a variety of factors, including the accused youth's age and alleged crime. For example, in Alabama, youth are considered juveniles until age 16, but judges can choose to send cases with offenders as young as 14 to adult criminal court. Some cases can be transferred via prosecutorial discretion. In these cases, the prosecutor has the option to determine which court—adult or juvenile—in which to charge the juvenile offender after considering the crime and the defendant's age. Finally, statutory exclusion laws give a state's adult criminal court exclusive jurisdiction over certain crimes, even if they involve juvenile offenders. For example, in

Pennsylvania, a child charged with homicide must be first charged in adult court. In Mississippi, a 13-year-old charged with a felony will be sent to adult court.

Other laws can influence whether a juvenile is tried in adult court. Some states have what are known as "once an adult, always an adult" laws, which require juveniles who have been previously tried in adult court to have all future cases heard in adult court, regardless of the alleged offense.[9] Reverse-waiver laws allow juveniles charged in adult court to petition the court to have their case transferred to juvenile court. The juvenile must provide reasons to argue for the transfer. In some states, juvenile courts have the power to give a juvenile an adult sentence, while adult courts can impose juvenile sentencing.

Depending on the laws of the state in which they are charged, juveniles can try to work with their lawyers to argue against being transferred to adult court.

IMPACT ON CRIME

Sending more juveniles to adult court for serious and

violent crimes was intended to deter youth crime. However,

prosecuting juveniles in adult court may actually do more

harm. A 2010 report from the University of California, Los

Angeles, School of Law's Juvenile Justice Project found

little evidence to support that trying juveniles as adults has

decreased juvenile violent crime. Instead, juveniles in many

states who were tried in adult court were more likely to

commit crimes in the future. According to the Centers for

Disease Control and Prevention, youth charged as adults

are nearly 35 percent more

likely to be arrested for future

offenses than those who are tried

as juveniles.[10]

When juveniles are

prosecuted and sentenced in

adult courts, they don't have

access to the rehabilitative

programs, education, and

treatments in the juvenile justice

system. Instead, they are placed

ADVANTAGES OF ADULT COURT

In some cases, there may be advantages for youth to be tried in adult court. First, juveniles tried in adult court have the right to a jury trial, something they don't have in juvenile court. Juries in adult court cases may be more sympathetic to a minor than a juvenile court judge would be. Also, court schedules are often packed, and jails are crowded. As a result, the adult court may be inclined to handle the juvenile's case more quickly and hand down a lighter sentence.

in adult criminal facilities, where they likely learn from the adult criminals around them. "As a crime control policy, placing more young people in [adult] criminal court appears to symbolize toughness more than it actually delivers toughness, and that symbol may have a high price," wrote researchers Jeffrey A. Butts and John K. Roman in a 2014 report about the effects of trying juveniles in adult court.[11]

LONG-TERM PROBLEMS

Numerous studies have shown that incarcerating youth in juvenile facilities can have negative effects. These include worsening existing mental illnesses, increasing the chances of reoffending, reducing the likelihood of returning to school, and reducing success at work.

Putting youth behind bars in adult prisons and jails can be even more harmful. Of all incarcerated people, juveniles who are held with adults have the highest risk of being sexually abused or suffering violence at the hands of other inmates or prison staff. In addition, they are 36 times more likely to commit suicide than youth held in juvenile facilities. Youth in adult facilities also have a higher risk of being placed in solitary confinement than their peers in juvenile facilities, according to the Prison Policy Initiative.[12] Youth offenders

A 15-year-old accused shooter hides his face as he is escorted into court, where authorities will decide whether he should be tried as an adult.

lose out on the educational and psychological programs juvenile facilities offer.

For incarcerated youth, these lifelong consequences are the result of decisions they made before they turned 18. Research has shown that the brains of adolescents are still developing and aren't fully formed. Therefore, many people believe that youth shouldn't be held to the same standard of responsibility as adults and shouldn't face the same punishments.

UNDERSTANDING THE ADOLESCENT BRAIN

In recent years, research has highlighted the differences between the brain functions of youth and adults. In particular, studies have shown that the adolescent brain doesn't fully develop until around age 25. Scientists have identified an area of the brain called the amygdala that controls immediate reactions such as fear and aggressive behavior. This area develops early. Another area of the brain, the frontal cortex, develops later. This area controls reasoning and helps people think before they act. The frontal cortex changes and matures into adulthood. These differences may help explain why the adolescent brain is more immature, emotional, and impulsive than a fully developed adult brain, which puts adolescents at a higher risk for committing delinquent acts. In addition, the adolescent brain is different in how it recognizes and responds to risks. Adolescents also differ from adults in how they're influenced by peers and in their capacity for learning and change. Other research shows that, if given time, most juvenile offenders outgrow delinquent behavior and become increasingly engaged in school and work as they grow into adulthood.

MAKING CHANGE

In the 2000s, many states realized that the strategy of trying juveniles as adults did little to prevent violent crime and instead created long-term problems for youth and society. A growing number of youth leaving adult prisons had psychological issues and were more likely to commit serious crimes in the future. In addition, incarceration is extremely expensive. According to one report by the Justice Policy Institute, incarcerating a single youth costs roughly $100,000 annually, as compared to $10,000 for a year of public school education.[13]

Since 2005, several states have implemented reforms to keep youth out of adult courts and prisons, according to the Campaign for Youth Justice. Some reform measures include raising the maximum age for juvenile court and creating alternatives to incarcerating juveniles in large adult detention centers. In New York, state officials created a task force to implement reforms such as a program to keep young offenders in their own communities. This allowed the offenders to focus on education and get treatment for mental health and substance abuse problems. Since these changes, the number of youth in New York state custody has dropped by 45 percent.[14] Arrests of youth have also dropped. In 2017, New York also passed legislation that changed how the state dealt with the majority of 16- and 17-year-old offenders, sending most of their cases to juvenile court instead of adult court. In juvenile court, adolescents receive much lighter sentences than in adult court. The new law also required counseling and other services for youth offenders.

DISCUSSION STARTERS

- Research has shown rehabilitation programs to be more helpful than incarceration for many juvenile offenders. Why do you think this is?
- Do you think there are any circumstances in which a juvenile can't be rehabilitated?
- Do you think 16- and 17-year-old offenders should be treated as adults or juveniles in court? Why?

CHAPTER SEVEN

LOCKED UP
FOR LIFE

Upon being arrested for a crime, many teenagers can't imagine
being incarcerated for the rest of their lives.

At age 17, Damion Todd was looking forward to his senior year of high school in Detroit, Michigan. He was the cocaptain of the school football team and hoped to play well enough to earn a college scholarship. But he also hung out with people who used guns. One night, some people shot at Todd and his friends after a party. In response, reportedly just to scare the people who'd shot at him, Todd repeatedly fired a gun into a crowd.[1] One of the bullets hit and killed 16-year-old Melody Rucker, and another injured her friend. Todd was found guilty of Rucker's murder and sentenced to life in prison. He became one of the thousands of youth serving life sentences in America's prisons for crimes they committed as juveniles.

Damion Todd was sentenced to life in prison at age 17 for fatally shooting a 16-year-old girl. Todd's original mug shot is on the left, while a photo of him at age 44 in 2017 is on the right.

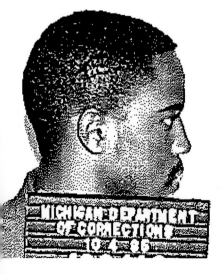

LIFE BEHIND BARS

The United States is one of few countries in the world that sentence juveniles to life in prison without the possibility of parole for crimes committed before age 18. The practice of locking up juveniles for life gained popularity in the 1980s and 1990s, when tough-on-crime policies led many states to pass laws to punish juvenile offenders as adults. Under these laws, juvenile offenders younger than 18 could be sentenced to live out the rest of their lives behind bars for serious, violent crimes such as homicide, rape, kidnapping, and armed robbery.

Today, nearly 12,000 people are serving a life or virtual life sentence for crimes committed before age 18. These inmates are in almost every state. Approximately 2,300 of them were sentenced to life without the possibility of parole. Another 7,300 are serving life sentences but are eligible for parole many years after their sentencing. In addition, about 2,100 juveniles are serving virtual life sentences, which are sentences of 50 years or more that extend beyond their expected life span.[2]

Amelia Bird, age 27, is currently serving two consecutive life sentences for her role as an accomplice in the murder of her mother and attempted murder of her father. Because the sentences are consecutive, Bird has very little chance of being released during her lifetime, even though she is technically eligible for parole. At age 17, Bird told her boyfriend that she had been abused by her brother and father. One night while she slept, Bird's boyfriend broke into her home and shot her parents, killing her mother and injuring her father. After she was arrested, Bird agreed to a plea deal with prosecutors to avoid the death penalty. She was sentenced to spend the rest of her life behind bars.

In recent years, a growing number of people and organizations have urged the criminal justice system to end the practice of giving juveniles life sentences. They argue that life sentences are too harsh for children who

BANNING THE DEATH PENALTY FOR JUVENILES

In 2005, the US Supreme Court banned the death penalty for juveniles in *Roper v. Simmons*. In Missouri, 17-year-old Christopher Simmons was convicted of murder and sentenced to death. His attorneys appealed his conviction and argued that imposing a death sentence for crimes committed when younger than 18 violated the Constitution's ban on cruel and unusual punishment. The Supreme Court ruled that defendants who were younger than 18 when they committed a crime couldn't be sentenced to death. At the time, the United States was the last country in the world that permitted minors to be executed for their crimes. In his majority opinion, Justice Anthony Kennedy noted that juveniles should be spared the death penalty because their immaturity can lead to rash decision-making. In addition, Justice Kennedy noted that minors are more vulnerable to peer pressure and are often unable to recognize and avoid circumstances in which crimes are likely to happen. Kennedy also explained that because juveniles are still developing, they can more successfully be rehabilitated to become law-abiding citizens.

committed crimes when they weren't developmentally
mature enough to understand the consequences of their
actions. "Unfortunately, adolescents, like adults, commit
horrible crimes and make terrible mistakes. And, like adults,
they should be held accountable—but in accordance with
their age, stage of development, and greater capacity for
rehabilitation. A sentence of life in prison is excessively harsh
for such young people, many of whom were themselves
victims of abuse or neglect," write Pat Arthur and Brittany
Armstrong from the National Center for Youth Law.[3]

SUPREME COURT RULINGS LIMIT JUVENILE LIFE SENTENCES

The US Supreme Court has issued rulings in several cases
involving juvenile life sentences. In 2010, the court ruled in
Graham v. Florida to ban the use of life without parole (LWOP)
for juveniles in nonhomicide cases. The court also ruled that
states must offer "some meaningful opportunity to obtain
release based on demonstrated maturity and rehabilitation,"
as Justice Anthony Kennedy wrote.[4]

In 2012, the Supreme Court turned its attention to
juveniles serving LWOP sentences for homicide. Some of
those offenders received their sentences because state

laws required a mandatory life sentence for certain serious crimes. The court ruled in *Miller v. Alabama* that mandatory sentencing of juveniles to life without the possibility of parole was unconstitutional. In reaching this decision, Justice Elena Kagan wrote that several factors should be considered in juvenile cases in order to determine fair and individual sentences. "Mandatory [LWOP] for a juvenile precludes consideration of his chronological age and its hallmark features—among them, immaturity, impetuosity, and failure to appreciate risks and consequences. It prevents taking into account the family and home environment that surrounds

It is difficult for parents and other family members to see juveniles convicted with the potential of serving long prison sentences.

him—and from which he cannot usually extricate himself—no matter how brutal or dysfunctional," she wrote.[5] Other factors Kagan believed should be considered in juvenile cases included the circumstances of the crime, incompetency of the juvenile in his or her own legal defense, and the possibility of rehabilitation.

The *Miller* ruling affected mandatory sentencing laws in many states. State courts struggled to apply *Miller* evenly, with some ruling that it was retroactive while others ruled that it was not. In 2016, the Supreme Court decided the issue and ruled in *Montgomery v. Louisiana* that the *Miller* decision could be applied retroactively. This meant that people who were already serving mandatory life-without-parole sentences would be given the chance to have a parole hearing or be resentenced. However, because the Supreme Court didn't completely ban juvenile life-without-parole sentences, states are still able to use this harsh punishment for juvenile offenders.

Eliminating mandatory life-without-parole sentences for juveniles didn't guarantee the release of everyone who had been given an LWOP sentence. Instead, it gave them the chance to have their cases reviewed for the possibility of parole. In these reviews, lower-level courts consider

A VICTIM'S PERSPECTIVE

Not everyone agrees that juveniles who commit heinous crimes deserve a second chance. At age 14, Evan Miller and another teen beat Miller's neighbor, Cole Cannon, with a baseball bat. They then set Cannon's trailer on fire while he was still inside. Cannon died from his injuries and smoke inhalation. A jury convicted Miller of murder and sentenced him to life without the possibility of parole. After the US Supreme Court ruled in his favor in *Miller v. Alabama*, Miller became eligible for a resentencing hearing. Candy Cheatham, the daughter of Miller's victim, says that his apology in court to her family was just empty words. She is angry that victims' families have to relive the pain of their loss during resentencing. "To bring this up and make the victims' families relive this, that's being cruel and unusual," she says.[7]

the unique circumstances of each defendant and case. In *Montgomery*, the Supreme Court ruled that "allowing those offenders to be considered for parole ensures that juveniles whose crimes reflected only transient immaturity—and who have since matured—will not be forced to serve a disproportionate sentence in violation of the Eighth Amendment."[6]

GETTING A SECOND CHANCE

The Supreme Court rulings have allowed hundreds of juveniles who were sentenced to life in prison to get the courts to take a second look at their cases. As a result, many defendants have been resentenced and released from prison. Now 49 years old, Damion Todd has been resentenced. After more than 30 years in prison, he became eligible for parole in 2018. Todd expresses regret over his actions as a teen and is thankful for a second chance. "It doesn't excuse what I did, but I'm not that kind of person anymore," he says.[8]

However, in some states, officials have delayed the review of juvenile life sentence cases or have pushed to keep youth offenders locked up for life. In Missouri, Timothy Willbanks received a sentence of 375 consecutive years in prison for kidnapping, robbery, and assault committed when he was 17. Recently, he challenged his sentence and argued that this lengthy term was substantively an LWOP sentence, which violated the *Graham v. Florida* ruling. The Missouri Supreme Court disagreed, saying that the Graham ruling applied to LWOP sentences specifically. It didn't apply to lengthy prison terms, even if they extended beyond a reasonable human life span. Additionally, the court reasoned that Willbanks would be eligible for parole at age 85.

STATES PUSH TO BAN LIFE SENTENCES

By 2018, 21 states and the District of Columbia had banned life sentences without the possibility of parole for juveniles. In a few other states, no juveniles are serving a life-without-parole sentence. Instead, many states have passed new laws with mandatory minimum sentences for youth, with a chance of parole. "There's been a very effective push by a number of juvenile-justice advocates to get more and more states to completely eliminate juvenile [LWOP], even for murder," says Douglas Berman, an Ohio State University law professor who specializes in criminal-sentencing issues. "At the legislative level, there have been more and more states coming online to completely eliminate it as a statutory matter."[9]

However, 29 states still allowed LWOP sentencing of juveniles as of 2018.[10] Youth may still be sentenced to discretionary, or nonmandatory, LWOP in homicide cases, as long as a court determines that the youth is not capable of being rehabilitated. In addition, many state laws that ban LWOP sentencing are prospective, meaning they only prevent future life sentences and don't affect people incarcerated for past LWOP sentences. For juveniles who have already been sentenced to discretionary LWOP, their fate rests in the hands of individual judges in the court system. These judges must consider complex cases and make decisions about whether it's appropriate to lock up people for the rest of their

100-YEAR SENTENCE

Maryland's highest court, the Court of Appeals, ruled in 2018 that a 100-year sentence for a juvenile for a single crime is unconstitutional. The court explained that a juvenile sentenced to 100 years would not be eligible for parole for 50 years. The court stated that such a sentence was equivalent to a life sentence and violated the US Constitution's Eighth Amendment, which bans cruel and unusual punishments.

lives for crimes committed as juveniles. These judges reach different conclusions in different cases.

Leigh Ann Zaepfel is serving a LWOP sentence in Oklahoma for murdering two people during a robbery in 1990, when she was 17. In 2018, Zaepfel was 45 and had served 28 years in prison. She believes she has become a completely different person than the troubled girl she was at 17. She hopes to have a chance at freedom someday. "I think mercy is important. . . . That's what Jesus taught: love, forgiveness and mercy," Zaepfel said during a prison interview. "So you can't define somebody by one mistake, without investigating, instead of putting everybody in a box."[11]

DISCUSSION STARTERS

- Do you think courts should be allowed to sentence a person to life in prison for a crime committed when they were younger than 18?
- How do you think courts should consider the perspective of victims and their families when sentencing violent juvenile offenders?
- Do you think there should be a maximum sentence for juvenile offenders?

CHAPTER EIGHT

REFORM EFFORTS

Many efforts to reform the juvenile justice system focus on education and rehabilitation, such as offering counseling and other programs to youth in the system.

S ince the early 2000s, efforts have increased to reform the juvenile justice system and refocus its priorities on education and rehabilitation. States are working to reduce the number of youth in correctional facilities by placing only the most chronic, violent offenders in secure facilities. The cost savings from reducing the number of youth in these facilities can then be used to fund reforms and programs that help youth stay out of the justice system.

KEEPING YOUTH IN THE JUVENILE SYSTEM

In the 1980s and 1990s, tough-on-crime policies and laws increased the number of youth transferred to the adult criminal justice system. In the adult system, youth lose access

An incarcerated youth participates in a small-engine class. These types of classes are part of efforts toward rehabilitation.

to programs and treatments that are critical for rehabilitation. As a result, many don't get the help they need.

Research has shown that keeping youth in the juvenile system, where they have access to more rehabilitative programs, provides better outcomes for them and society. Recognizing this, several states have implemented reforms to reduce the number of youth transferred to adult court. States such as Arizona, Indiana, Nevada, Missouri, and Ohio have limited the circumstances under which a juvenile can be transferred to adult court. Under these revised policies, courts can transfer only the most serious offenders to adult court. In Missouri, juveniles tried in adult court and found not guilty are now allowed to return to the juvenile system in any future cases instead of being required to stay in adult court for all future cases.

States such as California, Maryland, and Nebraska have passed legislation that requires juvenile court judges to consider a defendant's age, physical and mental health, and rehabilitation potential when deciding whether to transfer the case to adult court. Other states have eliminated the automatic transfer of adolescents to adult court. Still others have raised the maximum age at which a person is considered a juvenile in court.

TAKING OFF
THE SHACKLES

In 2005, the US Supreme Court ruled that shackling adult defendants during the sentencing portion of their trials would deny them due process, unless there was a specific, valid reason for the shackling. Shackles are physical restraints such as handcuffs, straitjackets, belly chains, and leg irons. The Supreme Court ruled that shackles created a visual image that the defendant was dangerous, which could influence the judge and jury and lead to harsher punishments. In the juvenile justice system, child advocates are working to have similar shackling reforms implemented. They argue that shackling juveniles in court can not only affect their cases but also have potentially damaging effects on the defendants. Putting children in shackles can cause intense shame and embarrassment, adding more trauma to youth who often have already experienced considerable trauma. It can lead to additional problem behaviors and may cause the youth to think of themselves as dangerous. Since 2005, several state legislatures and courts have reexamined the practice of shackling youth in the juvenile justice system when they have a court appearance. As of August 2018, 24 states and the District of Columbia had prohibited the use of unnecessary restraints in juvenile court.[1]

Many advocates say shackling juveniles in court can have negative psychological effects.

KEEPING KIDS OUT OF THE SYSTEM

Another goal of these reform efforts is to simply keep youth

out of the juvenile justice system entirely. According to

Dana Shoenberg from the Pew Charitable Trusts, putting

kids in the juvenile justice system may be doing more

harm than good over the long term. In general, she says,

community-based interventions lead to fewer rearrests

than putting kids in juvenile facilities. Even low-risk kids in a

secure juvenile facility are likely to be rearrested in the future.

"We do more harm by actually processing them through

the juvenile justice system than by taking a lighter touch,"

she said.[2]

V. Lowry Snow, a member of the Utah House of

Representatives who has worked on juvenile justice reform

YOUTH COURT

In an example of community-based interventions, youth courts are a type of diversion program that handles juvenile cases involving minor or status offenses and other problem behaviors. In youth court programs, youth participate in sentencing peers for offenses. Common youth court sentences include requiring the offender to apologize to the crime victim or participate in counseling or community service. Youth courts do not handle jail sentences. The programs aim to hold youth responsible for their behaviors while educating them about the legal and judicial systems and to motivate them to help solve community problems. Youth court programs can be administered by juvenile courts, juvenile probation departments, law enforcement, nonprofit organizations, and schools. Some youth courts have an adult judge and youth attorneys and jurors. Other models have youth fill all roles, including judge. Some youth courts use a panel of youth judges who make a sentencing decision. Today, there are more than 1,000 youth courts across the United States.[3]

in his state, agrees that preventing youth from entering the justice system is the best reform. Getting kids into programs that focus on rehabilitation and help them become productive adults can improve public safety, reduce rearrest rates, and reduce justice system costs. "One of the things I was most excited about was putting more focus on leaving our young people with their families in the home. Those are the best places for children to change behavior. We don't get the good outcomes we think we're getting by putting them in intensive treatment. In fact, we often get results that are worse. The best investment is on the front end," he says.[4]

ELIMINATING YOUTH PRISONS

As part of efforts to focus more on rehabilitation programs, some states are reducing their use of youth prisons.

In 2018, Connecticut governor Dannel Malloy announced the closure of a large state juvenile corrections facility, the Connecticut Juvenile Training School. In a statement, Malloy said, "In Connecticut, we're leading the nation in rethinking our approach to criminal justice, especially when it comes to the treatment of our young people. . . . The Connecticut Juvenile Training School . . . placed young boys in a prisonlike facility, making rehabilitation, healing, and

Dannel Malloy served as Connecticut's governor from 2011 to 2019.

growth more challenging." The facility's closure gives the state "an opportunity to create a system that better serves our young people and society as a whole," Malloy said.[5]

Connecticut's actions reflect the growing belief that the juvenile justice system's youth-prison model—which focuses on compliance, control, and punishment—contributes to youth trauma and reduces positive rehabilitation while doing little to improve public safety. Instead, more experts are recognizing that community-based approaches, rather than juvenile incarceration, are more effective at reducing rearrest rates, improving public safety, and controlling costs. These alternatives still hold youth accountable for their actions but provide them with better opportunities for rehabilitation.

Other states such as New Jersey, Virginia, and Wisconsin have also announced plans to close youth prisons as part of efforts to reform their juvenile justice systems. Instead of being incarcerated in large youth prisons, juveniles who need secure confinement will be sent to smaller therapeutic facilities that focus on rehabilitation. "The momentum is beginning to shift," says Patrick McCarthy of the Annie E. Casey Foundation. "Early-adopter states and localities are trying alternative approaches, and evidence-builders are showing the way."[6]

COMMUNITY-BASED ALTERNATIVES

Instead of confining youth in jail-like facilities, some states are developing more community-based alternatives to serve youth safely in their communities. Community-based alternatives are a wide range of programs and practices designed to reduce youth contact with the juvenile justice system and reduce juvenile incarceration. These alternatives include early-intervention programs, probation, restorative justice programs, diversion programs, evidence-based treatment programs such as family therapy, and more. Many of these alternatives are based on research and include evidence-based practices that have been extensively studied and found to consistently produce better results than traditional juvenile justice practices. Alternatives to justice system processing are open to a wide range of youth. Mostly, they are used for youth who have been charged with minor, nonviolent crimes, first offenses, or status offenses, as well as youth with mental health or substance abuse disorders.

The primary goals of community-based alternatives are to hold youth accountable for their actions while also providing them with the education, treatment, and support to keep them out of the criminal justice system in the future. For example, early-intervention programs are often designed for kids who are acting out in school or in the community by getting into fights, skipping school, running away, or committing other minor or status offenses. Their behavior may be caused by a variety of issues including mental health disorders, substance abuse, learning deficits, trauma, and family troubles. By addressing the underlying issues, these programs help kids stay out of the justice system.

RESTORATIVE JUSTICE

Restorative justice focuses on crime as an offense against an individual and a community. As such, restorative justice focuses on the needs of the victims, offenders, and community over punishment of the offender. Offenders are encouraged to take responsibility for their actions, make amends, and attempt to repair the harm they have done to others. The process helps youth offenders better understand the consequences of their actions and helps prevent future crime. Research has shown that restorative justice programs that promote dialogue between youth offenders and their victims are more effective at holding offenders accountable and helping victims heal.

WORKING TOGETHER

In several states, government leaders have launched multiyear efforts to improve their juvenile justice systems. For example, Georgia has implemented many reforms since 2013. These include reducing mandatory minimum sentences and banning residential commitment for status offenses and some low-level misdemeanor crimes. The state also established a grant program for counties to help them reduce the number of juveniles sent to state custody.

These reforms have been successful. As of 2017, Georgia had seen the number of incarcerated youth drop by 36 percent. Total commitments to the state's Department of Juvenile Justice have dropped by nearly half.[7] In addition, the state closed three juvenile commitment facilities and designated $30 million for community-based sentencing programs. With these new programs, judges across the state have

HELPING YOUTH IN GEORGIA

In Chatham County, Georgia, the juvenile court has implemented a new program designed to help young people connect to work and avoid confinement. In the Work Readiness Enrichment Program, several local government agencies and community organizations have come together to help boys ages 14 to 16 who have been charged with a felony or multiple property crimes and who have fallen significantly behind in school. The eight- to ten-week program addresses several areas, including educational needs, work readiness skills, parenting skills, and behavioral health. It also teaches financial literacy and connects older youth to job opportunities.

the ability to send juveniles to at least one evidence-based treatment program.

In 2017, Utah's governor signed new juvenile justice legislation designed to reduce the number of youth in out-of-home placements by 47 percent over the next five years and to expand early-intervention and evidence-based programs for Utah youth. Some of the legislation's provisions include requiring cases involving misdemeanors, status offenses, and other minor crimes to be diverted before court if the youth has had limited previous involvement with the justice system. It also establishes time limits for out-of-home placements, except in cases involving serious offenses or when youth are completing essential out-of-home treatment. The legislation also sets limits for court-ordered fines and fees and expands state funding for evidence-based, in-home community services.

Some states are putting more money toward treatment programs in hopes of decreasing juvenile incarceration.

According to Jake Horowitz, director of research
and policy for the Pew Charitable Trusts' public safety
performance project, when appropriate reforms are put in
place, the benefits are significant. "The bottom line," he says,
"is that states don't need more correctional space to achieve
less crime. In fact, they've protected public safety with
dramatically lower levels of incarceration by aligning policies
and resources with what the research indicates will produce
the highest return on their juvenile justice investments."[8]
While reforms have been made in many areas, there is still
more work to be done. As lawmakers, advocates, and others
learn which practices are most effective in juvenile justice,
reform efforts will continue to improve the juvenile justice
system for all youth.

DISCUSSION STARTERS

- How does restorative justice differ from traditional punishment-based justice? Do you think all juvenile sentences should include an element of restorative justice?
- Why do you think community-based alternatives have been shown to be more successful in many cases than traditional punishment? In what circumstances would they not be appropriate?
- What impact do you think early-intervention programs have on the juvenile justice system?

ESSENTIAL FACTS

SIGNIFICANT EVENTS

- In 1899, the first juvenile court in the United States was founded in Cook County, Illinois.

- In 1967, the US Supreme Court established juvenile trial rights via *In re Gault*. The court ruled that in cases that could end in a juvenile being incarcerated, the juvenile had many of the same trial rights as an adult, including the right to an attorney, the right to question witnesses, and the right against self-incrimination.

- In the late 1980s and early 1990s, state legislators passed "tough-on-crime" policies that allowed prosecutors to more easily move youth from the juvenile justice system to adult criminal court for trial and punishment.

- In 2005, the Supreme Court banned the death penalty for juveniles.

- In 2010, the Supreme Court banned life-without-parole sentences for juveniles who committed nonhomicide crimes. The court followed up this ruling with a decision in 2012 that stated sentencing a juvenile to a mandatory life-without-parole sentence was unconstitutional.

KEY PLAYERS

- Gerald Gault was sentenced to six years in a juvenile facility at 15 years old for making indecent phone calls. His case, *In re Gault*, led to youth in the juvenile justice system having many of the same due process rights as adults.

- Tristin Kurilla was ten years old when he was charged with the murder of an elderly woman. His case highlighted many issues surrounding juvenile justice.

- Supreme Court Justice Anthony Kennedy ruled in several cases between 2010 and 2016 that limited juvenile life-without-parole sentences.

IMPACT ON SOCIETY

When children commit crimes, especially violent offenses, how should they be treated by the criminal justice system? In the United States, there is a separate justice system for juveniles designed to help rehabilitate youth offenders and help them become productive, law-abiding adults in society. The juvenile justice system is essential because youth offenders are much different—developmentally, emotionally, and intellectually—than adult offenders. Research shows that because of their young age, juveniles have a better chance of successful rehabilitation. As violent crime increased in the 1980s and 1990s, many states implemented tougher laws that made it easier to transfer youth offenders to the adult criminal justice system. However, as crime rates have dropped, many state governments are attempting to reform their juvenile justice systems and implement alternatives to help youth stay out of the justice system. By understanding how juvenile justice works and the effect it can have on youth across the country, people can work to make changes to help juvenile offenders become responsible adults while still ensuring public safety.

QUOTE

"Unfortunately, adolescents, like adults, commit horrible crimes and make terrible mistakes. And, like adults, they should be held accountable—but in accordance with their age, stage of development, and greater capacity for rehabilitation."

—Pat Arthur and Brittany Armstrong, in a report from the National Center for Youth Law

GLOSSARY

autopsy
The examination of a body after death to determine the cause of death.

correctional
Relating to the punishment of criminals.

delinquent
A young person who shows a tendency to commit a crime, often minor crimes.

detention
The act of holding a person in custody.

disparity
A large difference.

due process
The legal requirement that the state must respect all legal rights that are owed to a person.

felony
A crime more serious than a misdemeanor, usually punishable by imprisonment.

homicide
When one person kills another person.

incarceration
The state of being in prison.

jurisdiction
A certain area within which a group has authority to make a legal decision or take legal action.

life sentence
A sentence for a crime that requires people to be imprisoned for the rest of their natural life.

misdemeanor

A crime with less serious penalties than those assessed for a felony.

parole

Early release from prison because of good behavior under the condition that good behavior continue.

probable cause

The legal requirement that law enforcement must have an adequate reason based on facts to arrest someone, search or seize property, or obtain a warrant.

probation

The release of a prisoner who remains under supervision instead of incarceration.

proceedings

The activities and hearings of a legal body such as a court.

reform

A change.

rehabilitate

To use education or therapy to return someone to a normal life after criminal activity or substance abuse.

stigma

A set of negative and often unfair beliefs that a society or group of people has about something.

waiver

Permission to ignore rules.

ADDITIONAL RESOURCES

SELECTED BIBLIOGRAPHY

Rovner, Joshua. "Racial Disparities in Youth Commitments and Arrests." *Sentencing Project*, 1 April 2016. sentencingproject.org. Accessed 26 Dec. 2018.

Sawyer, Wendy. "Youth Confinement: The Whole Pie." *Prison Policy Initiative*, 27 Feb. 2018, prisonpolicy.org. Accessed 26 Dec. 2018.

"The History of Juvenile Justice." *American Bar Association*, n.d., americanbar.org. Accessed 26 Dec. 2018.

"Youth in the Justice System." *Juvenile Law Center*, n.d., jlc.org. Accessed 26 Dec. 2018.

FURTHER READINGS

Harris, Duchess, and Rebecca Morris. *The History of Law Enforcement.* Abdo, 2020.

Micklos, John. *True Stories of Teen Prisoners*. Cavendish Square, 2018.

ONLINE RESOURCES

Booklinks
NONFICTION NETWORK
FREE! ONLINE NONFICTION RESOURCES

To learn more about the juvenile justice system, visit **abdobooklinks.com**. These links are routinely monitored and updated to provide the most current information available.

MORE INFORMATION

For more information on this subject, contact or visit the following organizations:

The Annie E. Casey Foundation
701 St. Paul St.
Baltimore, MD 21202
410-547-6600
aecf.org

The Annie E. Casey Foundation is a private philanthropic organization focused on developing a brighter future for at-risk children, including those involved in the juvenile justice system.

Center on Juvenile and Criminal Justice
424 Guerrero St., Suite A
San Francisco, CA 94110
415-621-5661
cjcj.org

The Center on Juvenile and Criminal Justice is a nonprofit, nonpartisan organization that works to promote a balanced criminal justice system designed to reduce incarceration and enhance long-term public safety.

Office of Juvenile Justice and Delinquency Prevention
810 Seventh St. NW
Washington, DC 20531
202-307-5911
ojjdp.gov

The Office of Juvenile Justice and Delinquency Prevention is part of the US Department of Justice. It supports the efforts of states, Native American tribes, and local governments to develop and implement effective and fair juvenile justice systems that enhance public safety, hold youth accountable to both crime victims and communities, and empower youth to live productive, law-abiding lives.

SOURCE NOTES

CHAPTER 1. WHEN CHILDREN COMMIT CRIMES

1. Ray Sanchez. "Cops: Boy, 10, Kills Woman, 90, for Yelling at Him," *CNN*, 14 Oct. 2014, cnn.com. Accessed 22 Jan. 2019.

2. Sanchez, "Cops: Boy, 10, Kills Woman."

3. Sanchez, "Cops: Boy, 10, Kills Woman."

4. Christopher Moraff. "10-Year-Old Murder Defendant Shows Failure of US Juvenile Justice System." *Daily Beast*, 18 Oct. 2014, thedailybeast.com. Accessed 22 Jan. 2019.

5. Meg Wagner. "Pennsylvania 10-Year-Old Accused of Killing 90-Year-Old Misses His Mom, Finds Adult Jail Scary: Lawyer." *New York Daily News*, 11 Dec. 2014, nydailynews.com. Accessed 22 Jan. 2019.

6. Kathleen Michon. "Juvenile Law: Status Offenses." *Nolo*, n.d., nolo.com. Accessed 22 Jan. 2019.

7. "The Reasons for Treating Juveniles Differently." *Frontline*, n.d., pbs.org. Accessed 22 Jan. 2019.

8. Moraff, "10-Year-Old Murder Defendant."

9. Moraff, "10-Year-Old Murder Defendant."

10. Stacy Lange. "10-Year-Old Accused Killer Moved to Juvenile Court." *WNEP*, 5 Jan. 2015, WNEP.com. Accessed 22 Jan. 2019.

CHAPTER 2. HISTORY OF THE JUVENILE JUSTICE SYSTEM

1. Jake Horowitz and Arna Carlock. "Juvenile Commitment Rate Falls by Half Nationally in 10 Years." *Pew*, 18 Sept. 2017, pewtrusts.org. Accessed 22 Jan. 2019.

CHAPTER 3. JUVENILE INCARCERATION

1. Wendy Sawyer. "Youth Confinement: The Whole Pie." *Prison Policy Initiative*, 27 Feb. 2018, prisonpolicy.org. Accessed 22 Jan. 2019.

2. Sawyer, "Youth Confinement: The Whole Pie."

3. Timothy Beryl Bland. "Cottage System." *The Encyclopedia of Juvenile Delinquency and Justice*. Wiley, 2017. *Wiley Online Library*. Accessed 22 Jan. 2019.

4. Sawyer, "Youth Confinement: The Whole Pie."

5. Sawyer, "Youth Confinement: The Whole Pie."

6. Sawyer, "Youth Confinement: The Whole Pie."

7. Patrick McCarthy, Vincent Schiraldi, and Miriam Shark. "The Future of Youth Justice: A Community-Based Alternative to the Youth Prison Model." *New Thinking in Community Corrections*, no. 2, Oct. 2016, ncjrs.gov. Accessed 22 Jan. 2019.

8. Sawyer, "Youth Confinement: The Whole Pie."

9. Sawyer, "Youth Confinement: The Whole Pie."

10. Sawyer, "Youth Confinement: The Whole Pie."

11. "The Harms of Juvenile Detention." *National Juvenile Defender Center*, n.d., njdc.info. Accessed 22 Jan. 2019.

12. Andrew M. Seaman. "Being Incarcerated as a Juvenile Tied to Poor Health Years Later." *Reuters*, 23 Jan. 2017, reuters.com. Accessed 22 Jan. 2019.

13. Richard A. Mendel. "Maltreatment of Youth in US Juvenile Corrections Facilities: An Update." *Annie E. Casey Foundation*, 2015, aecf.org. Accessed 22 Jan. 2019.

14. Sarah Hockenberry. "Juveniles in Residential Placement, 2015." *Juvenile Justice Statistics: National Report Series Bulletin*, Jan. 2018, ojjdp.gov. Accessed 22 Jan. 2019.

15. Mendel, "Maltreatment of Youth."

16. Patrick McCarthy and Vincent Schiraldi. "Youth Prisons Don't Reform, They Damage: Column." *USA Today*, 27 Oct. 2016, usatoday.com. Accessed 22 Jan. 2019.

17. Megan Cottrell. "Locking Up Children Just Doesn't Work, a Study Says." *Chicago Reporter: Chicago Muckrakers*, 10 Oct. 2011, chicagonow.com. Accessed 22 Jan. 2019.

CHAPTER 4. GENDER DISPARITIES

1. Chandlee Johnson Kuhn. "Gender Disparities in the Juvenile Justice System." *Coalition for Juvenile Justice*, 23 Oct. 2013, juvjustice.org. Accessed 22 Jan. 2019.

2. "Girls, Status Offenses and the Need for a Less Punitive and More Empowering Approach." *Emerging Issues Policy Series,* no. 1, Fall 2013, juvjustice.org. Accessed 22 Jan. 2019.

3. Yasmin Vafa et al. "Beyond the Walls: A Look at Girls in DC's Juvenile Justice System." *Rights4Girls and the Georgetown Juvenile Justice Initiative*, Mar. 2018, rights4girls.org. Accessed 22 Jan. 2019.

4. Donna M. Bishop and Charles E. Frazier. "Gender Bias in Juvenile Justice Processing." *Journal of Criminal Law and Criminology*, vol. 82, issue 4, Winter 1992. *Northwestern University School of Law Scholarly Commons*. Accessed 22 Jan. 2019.

5. Wendy Sawyer. "Youth Confinement: The Whole Pie." *Prison Policy Initiative*, 27 Feb. 2018, prisonpolicy.org. Accessed 22 Jan. 2019.

6. Vafa et al., "Beyond the Walls."

7. Vafa et al., "Beyond the Walls."

8. Vafa et al., "Beyond the Walls."

9. Vafa et al., "Beyond the Walls."

10. Teresa Wiltz. "States Grapple with Girls in the Juvenile Justice System." *Pew*, 25 Nov. 2015, pewtrusts.org. Accessed 22 Jan. 2019.

11. Vafa et al., "Beyond the Walls."

12. Vafa et al., "Beyond the Walls."

13. Timothy Williams. "History of Abuse Seen in Many Girls in Juvenile System." *New York Times*, 9 July 2015, nytimes.com. Accessed 22 Jan. 2019.

14. Malika Saada Saar et al. "The Sexual Abuse to Prison Pipeline: The Girls' Story." *Human Rights Project for Girls*, n.d., rights4girls.org. Accessed 22 Jan. 2019.

SOURCE NOTES CONTINUED

CHAPTER 5. RACE AND JUVENILE JUSTICE

1. Joshua Rovner. "Racial Disparities in Youth Commitments and Arrests." *Sentencing Project*, 1 Apr. 2016, sentencingproject.org. Accessed 22 Jan. 2019.

2. "Racial and Ethnic Disparities in the Juvenile Justice System." *National Conference of State Legislatures*, 11 Jan. 2018, ncsl.org. Accessed 22 Jan. 2019.

3. Rovner, "Racial Disparities."

4. Rovner, "Racial Disparities."

5. Rovner, "Racial Disparities."

6. Sara Tiano. "In California, Data Shows a Widening Racial Gap as Juvenile Incarceration Has Declined." *Chronicle of Social Change*, 28 Nov. 2017, chronicalofsocialchange.org. Accessed 22 Jan. 2019.

7. Tiano, "In California, Data Shows a Widening Racial Gap."

8. German Lopez. "20 States Still Haven't Outlawed Racial Profiling. Has Yours?" *Vox*, 26 Sept. 2014, vox.com. Accessed 22 Jan. 2019.

CHAPTER 6. TRIED AS ADULTS

1. Renata Sago. "Charging Youths as Adults Can Be a 'Cruel Wake-Up Call.' Is There Another Way?" *National Public Radio*, 15 Aug. 2017, npr.org. Accessed 22 Jan. 2019.

2. Sago, "Charging Youths as Adults."

3. "Keep Youth Out of Adult Courts, Jails, and Prisons." *National Juvenile Justice Network*, n.d., njjn.org. Accessed 22 Jan. 2019.

4. "Keep Youth Out of Adult Courts, Jails, and Prisons."

5. Sago, "Charging Youths as Adults."

6. "Children in Adult Jails." *Economist*, 28 Mar. 2015, economist.com. Accessed 22 Jan. 2019.

7. Wendy Sawyer. "Youth Confinement: The Whole Pie." *Prison Policy Initiative*, 27 Feb. 2018, prisonpolicy.org. Accessed 22 Jan. 2019.

8. "Fact Sheet: Direct File." *Campaign for Youth Justice*, 12 Feb. 2018, campaignforyouthjustice.org. Accessed 22 Jan. 2019.

9. Nicole Scialabba. "Should Juveniles Be Charged as Adults in the Criminal Justice System?" *American Bar Association*, 3 Oct. 2016, americanbar.org. Accessed 22 Jan. 2019.

10. "Children in Adult Jails."

11. Jeffrey A. Butts and John K. Roman. "Line Drawing: Raising the Minimum Age of Criminal Court Jurisdiction in New York." *John Jay College of Criminal Justice*, Feb. 2014. *Semantic Scholar*, pdfs.semanticscholar.org. Accessed 22 Jan. 2019.

12. Maddie Troilo. "Locking Up Youth with Adults: An Update." *Prison Policy Initiative*, 27 Feb. 2018, prisonpolicy.org. Accessed 22 Jan. 2019.

13. Matthew Green. "Should Kids Who Commit Serious Crimes Be Sentenced as Adults?" *KQED Education*, 25 Mar. 2016, kqed.org. Accessed 22 Jan. 2019.

14. Sarah Childress. "Why States Are Changing Course on Juvenile Crime." *Frontline*, 17 Dec. 2014, pbs.org. Accessed 22 Jan. 2019.

CHAPTER 7. LOCKED UP FOR LIFE

1. Sharon Cohen. "The Soon-to-Be Parolee." *Associated Press*, 31 July 2017, ap.org. Accessed 22 Jan. 2019.

2. Ashely Nellis. "Still Life: America's Increasing Use of Life and Long-Term Sentences." *Sentencing Project*, 3 May 2017, sentencingproject.org. Accessed 22 Jan. 2019.

3. Pat Arthur and Brittany Star Armstrong. "Locked Away Forever: The Case against Juvenile Life without Parole." *National Center for Youth Law*, n.d., youthlaw.org. Accessed 22 Jan. 2019.

4. Matt Ford. "The Reckoning over Young Prisoners Serving Life without Parole." *Atlantic*, 14 July 2017, theatlantic.com. Accessed 22 Jan. 2019.

5. Ford, "The Reckoning."

6. Josh Rovner. "Juvenile Life without Parole: An Overview." *Sentencing Project*, 22 Oct. 2018, sentencingproject.org. Accessed 22 Jan. 2019.

7. Sharon Cohen and Adam Geller. "Parole for Young Lifers Inconsistent across US." *Associated Press*, 31 July 2017, ap.org. Accessed 22 Jan. 2019.

8. Cohen, "The Soon-to-Be Parolee."

9. Ford, "The Reckoning."

10. Rovner, "Juvenile Life without Parole."

11. "Ruling Brings Parole Chance for Those Who Killed as Children." *MSN*, 3 Oct. 2018, msn.com. Accessed 22 Jan. 2019.

CHAPTER 8. REFORM EFFORTS

1. Anne Teigen. "States That Limit or Prohibit Juvenile Shackling and Solitary Confinement." *National Conference of State Legislatures*, 16 Aug. 2018, ncsl.org. Accessed 22 Jan. 2019.

2. Jane Carroll Andrade. "Reforming the Juvenile Justice System by Keeping Kids Out of It." *National Conference of State Legislatures*, 2 Aug. 2018, ncsl.org. Accessed 22 Jan. 2019.

3. "Youth Courts: Facts and Stats." *National Association of Youth Courts*, n.d., youthcourt.net. Accessed 22 Jan. 2019.

4. Andrade, "Reforming the Juvenile Justice System."

5. Josh Kovner. "Connecticut Juvenile Training School Closes." *Hartford Courant*, 12 April 2018, courant.com. Accessed 31 Jan. 2019.

6. "Momentum Builds in States to End the Youth Prison Model." *Annie E. Casey Foundation*, 15 Jan. 2018, aecf.org. Accessed 22 Jan. 2019.

7. Jake Horowitz. "States Take the Lead on Juvenile Justice Reform." *Pew*, 11 May 2017, pewtrusts.org. Accessed 22 Jan. 2019.

8. Horowitz, "States Take the Lead."

INDEX

ABOUT THE AUTHORS

DUCHESS HARRIS, JD, PHD

Dr. Harris is a professor of American Studies at Macalester College and curator of the Duchess Harris Collection of ABDO books. She is also the coauthor of the titles in the collection, which features popular selections such as *Hidden Human Computers: The Black Women of NASA* and series including News Literacy and Being Female in America.

Before working with ABDO, Dr. Harris authored several other books on the topics of race, culture, and American history. She served as an associate editor for *Litigation News*, the American Bar Association Section of Litigation's quarterly flagship publication, and was the first editor in chief of *Law Raza*, an interactive online journal covering race and the law, published at William Mitchell College of Law. She has earned a PhD in American Studies from the University of Minnesota and a JD from William Mitchell College of Law.

CARLA MOONEY

Carla Mooney is a graduate of the University of Pennsylvania. She writes for young people and is the author of many books for young adults and children. Mooney enjoys learning about social issues and making the world a more inclusive place for all people.